FROM WAX To Crayon

A Photo Essay

by Michael H. Forman

Children's Press

A Division of Scholastic Inc.
New York • Toronto • London • Auckland • Sydney
Mexico City • New Delhi • Hong Kong
Danbury, Connecticut

Created and Developed by The Learning Source

Designed by Josh Simons

Acknowledgments: We would like to thank Binney & Smith, the producers of Crayola crayons, the Children's Aid Society, and the other organizations who provided technical assistance with this project. Their help is greatly appreciated.

Illustrations: Aliza Simons: cover, 5 (right); Casey Simons: 5 (botttom left), 30 (right); Dyani Holiday: 31 (right); Emily Egan: 1; Gabriel Barth-Maron: 30 (left); Noah Forman: 5 (top); Rachel & Ariel Ball: 31 (left); Tammy Christian: 30 (center).

Photo Credits: Binney & Smith: 2-3, 8, 10-11, 13 (right), 14-27, back cover; Ken Karp: 8 (inset), 28-29: Robert Egan: 4-7; Sun Chemical Corporation: 13 (left).

Note: The actual crayon-making process often varies from manufacturer to manufacturer. The facts and details included in this book are representative of one of the most common ways of producing crayons today.

Library of Congress Cataloging-in-Publication Data

Forman, Michael H.

From wax to crayon / by Michael H. Forman.

p. cm. — (Changes)

Summary: Describes how crayons are made, inspected, wrapped, sorted, and packed for use in drawing and coloring just about anything on earth.

ISBN 0-516-20708-3 (lib. bdg.) ISBN 0-516-20360-6 (pbk.)

1. Crayons — Juvenile literature. [1. Crayons.] I. Title. II. Series: Changes (New York, N.Y.)

TS1268.F67 1997

741.2'3—dc21

96-51022 CIP

AC

Printed in China

11 R 10 09 08 62

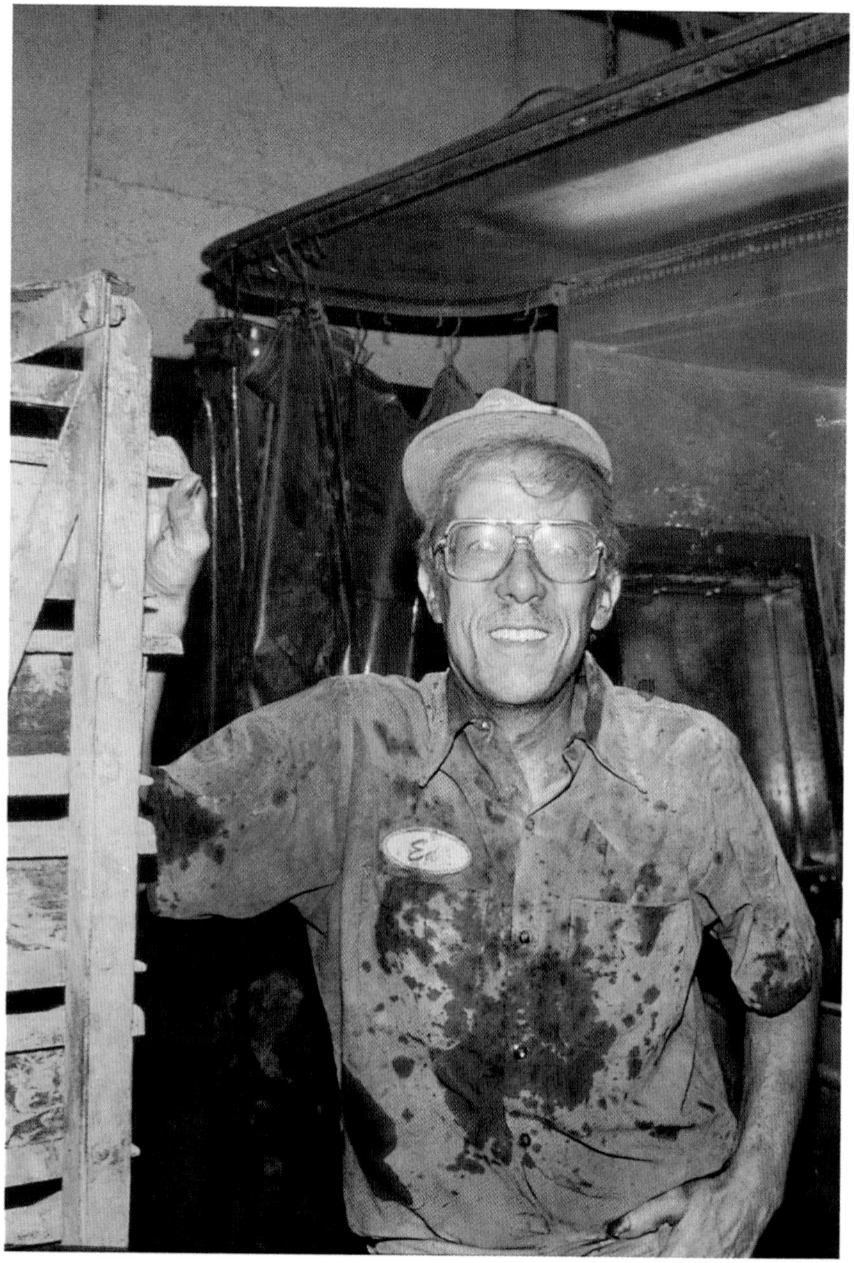

Where will your crayons take you?
Will they lead you to tall, crowded cities
or into thick, dark forests
or for visits beneath the sea?

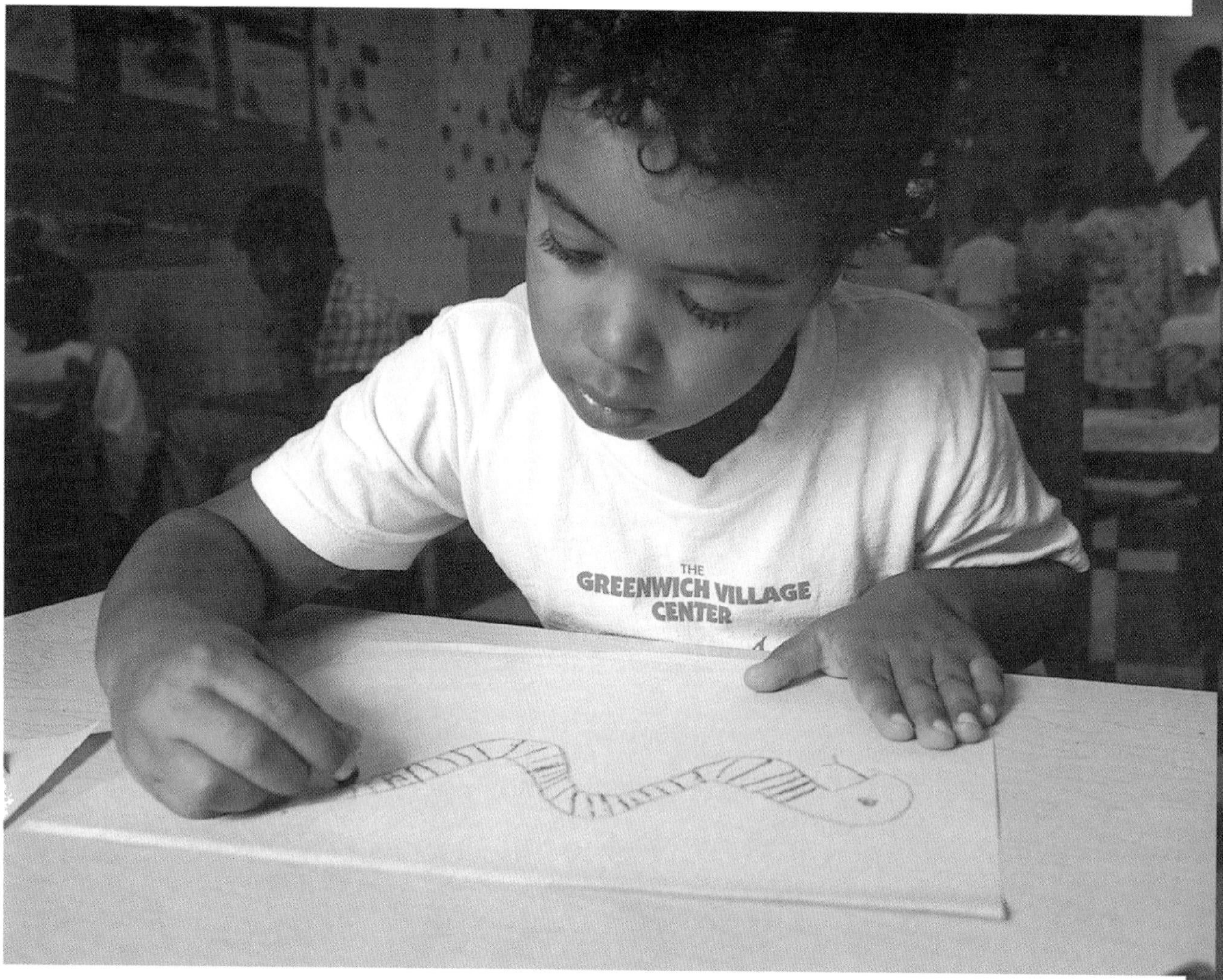

With crayons you can travel anywhere. Just bring along your imagination and lots of different colors.

CRAYONS

But where do crayons come from?

Crayons begin with wax. So, outside the crayon factory, tanks of clear, gooey wax stand, waiting for color.

Meanwhile, at the color mill, the primary colors—red, blue, and yellow—are made from chemicals.

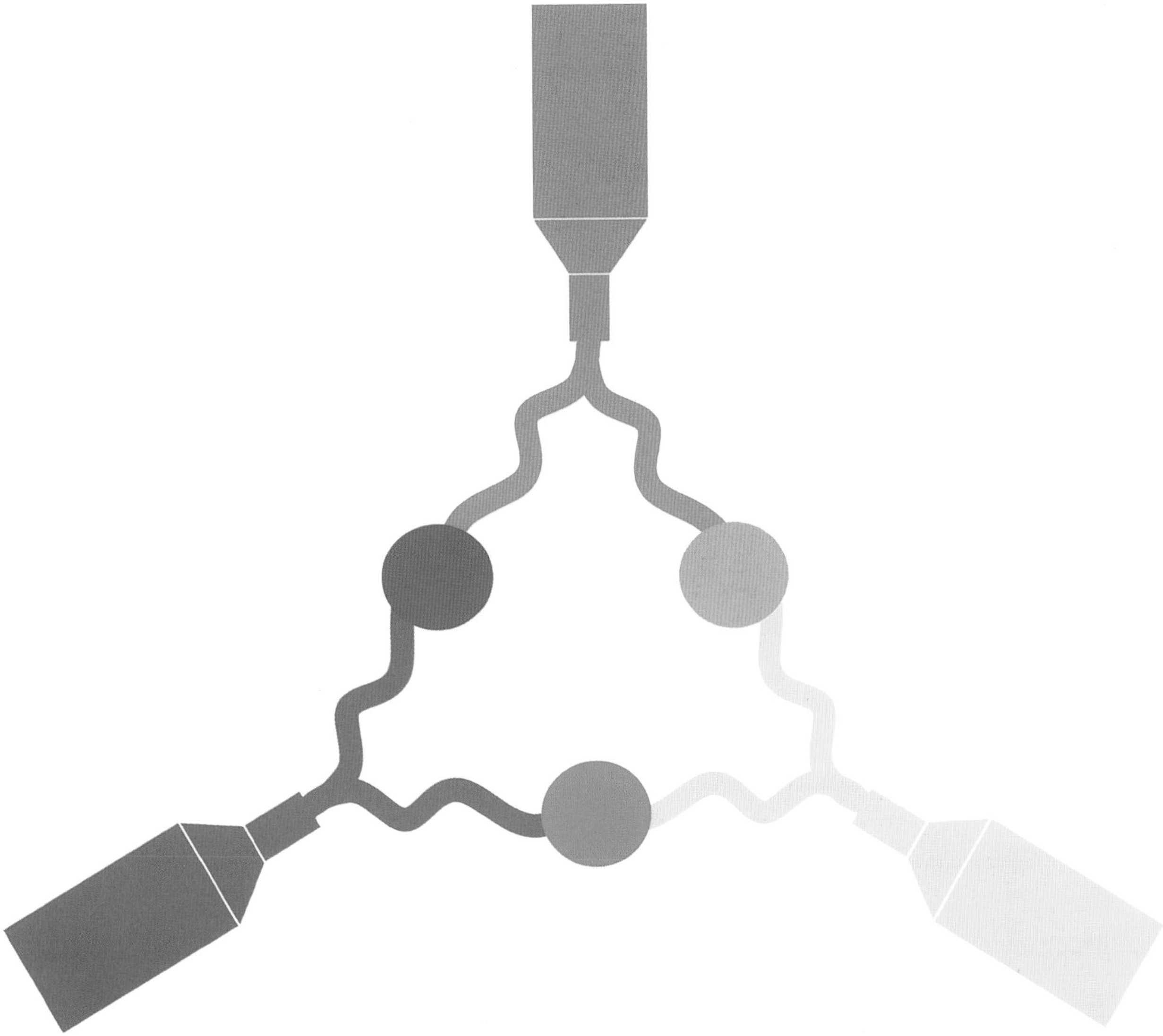

The primary colors are then mixed together in different ways to create many other colors.

Once a color looks right, its mixture is baked in a special oven, called a kiln.

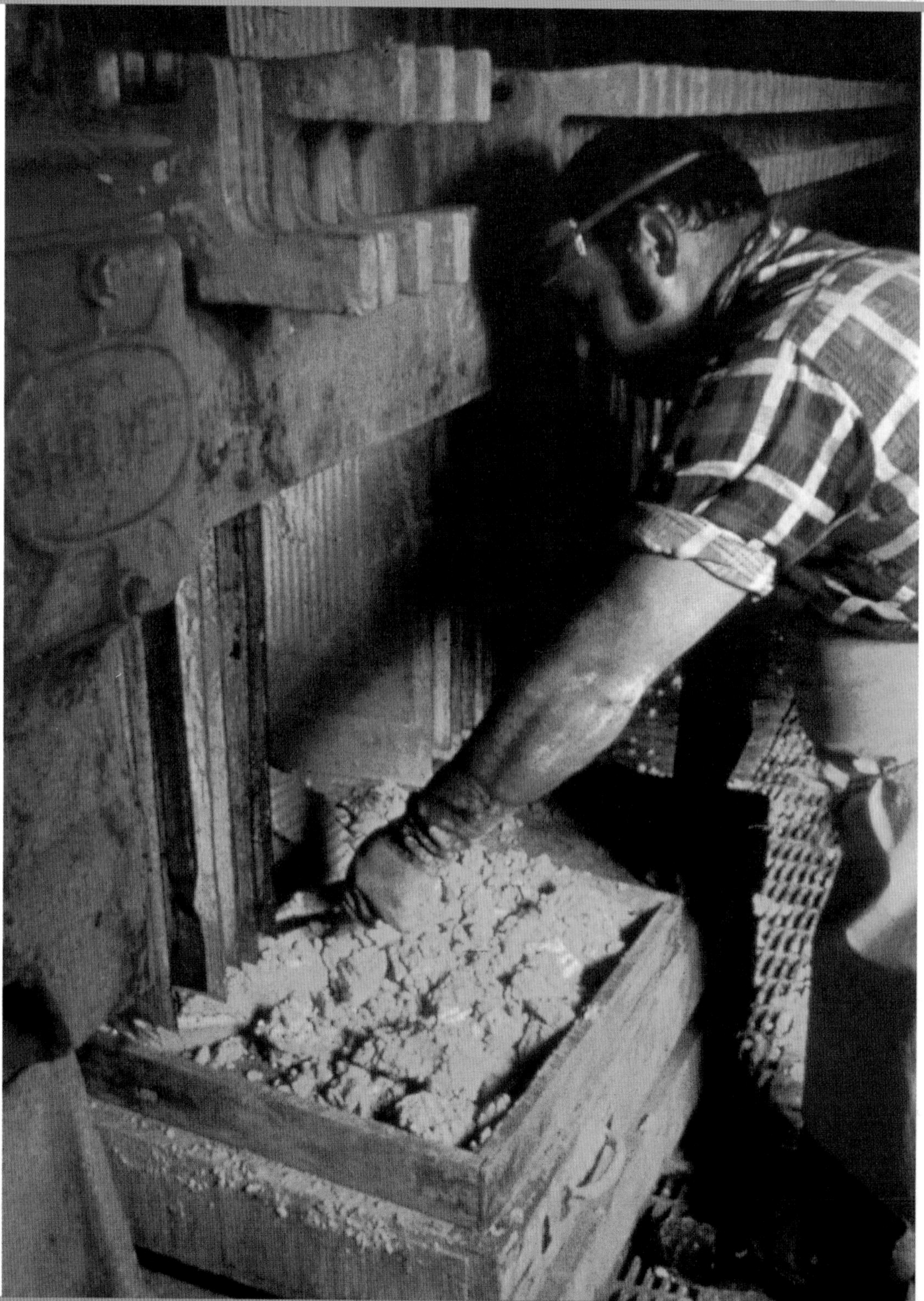

Hours later, hard color cakes are removed from the kiln . . .

. . . and ground into fine powder by a pulverizing machine.

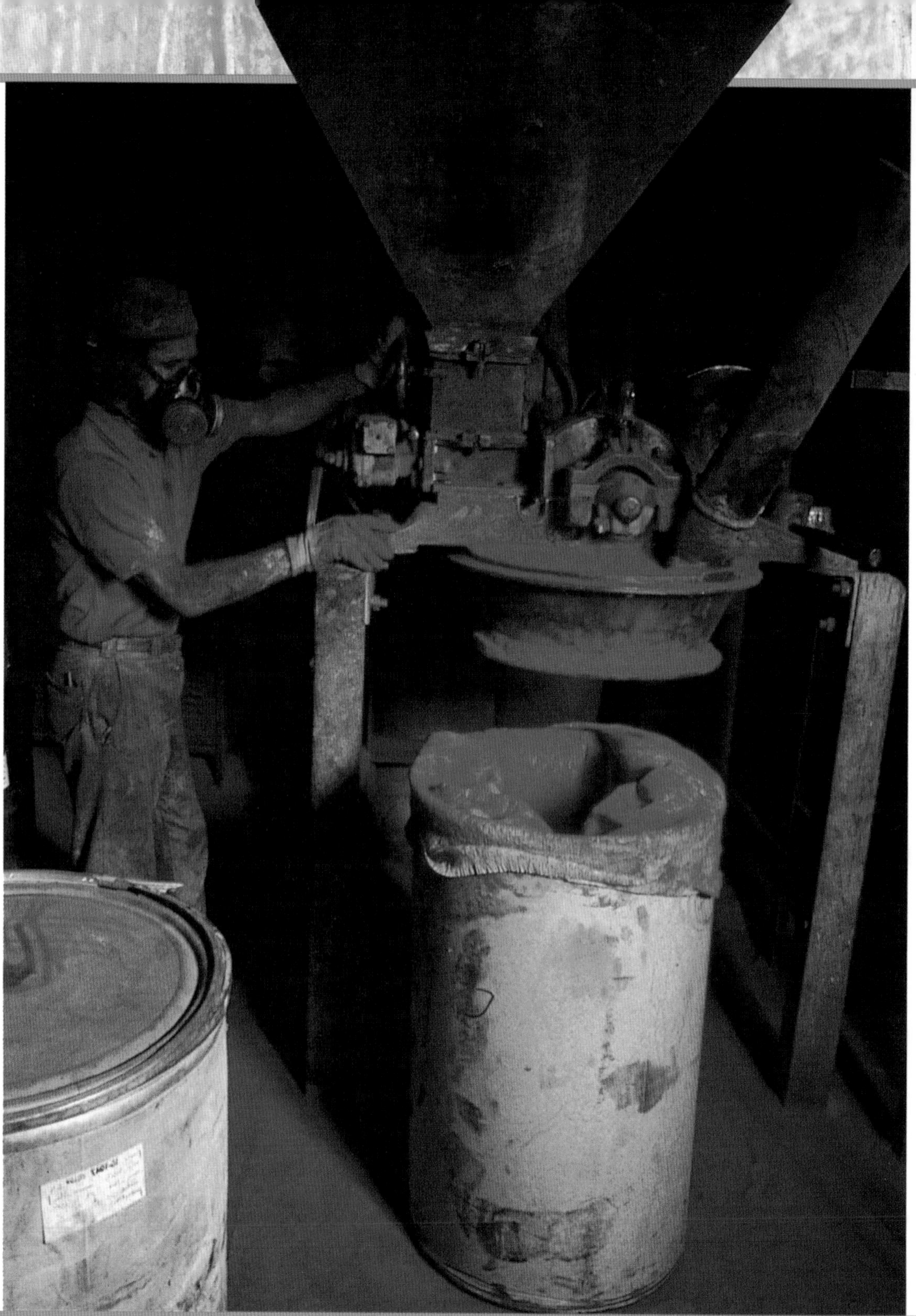

The colored powder, called pigment, is packed into bags and sent off to the crayon factory.

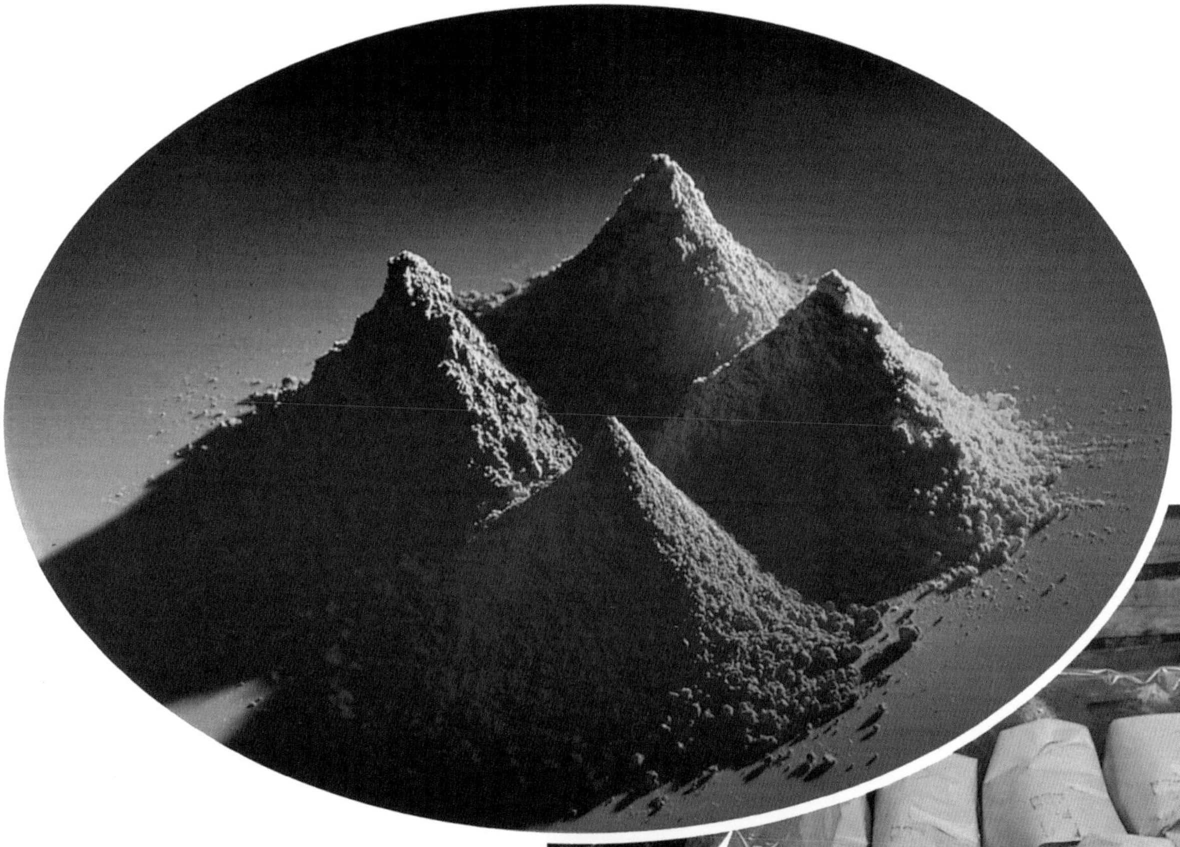

There, in big vats, the pigments are mixed with very hot, liquid wax.

Each mixture of wax and pigment must be blended over and over. Otherwise, one end of a crayon could come out a different color than the other end.

The newly colored wax is poured over molds and stirred to keep air bubbles from forming. A bubble inside a crayon might cause it to break later on.

Soon the wax hardens into these familiar shapes.

The crayons must cool for a while. Then they are removed from the molds . . .

. . . and checked for chips and dents. After all, no one wants new crayons that are already broken.

A machine wraps and labels each crayon . . .

. . . and boxes it with others that are exactly the same.
But hundreds of crayons of the same color aren't much fun.

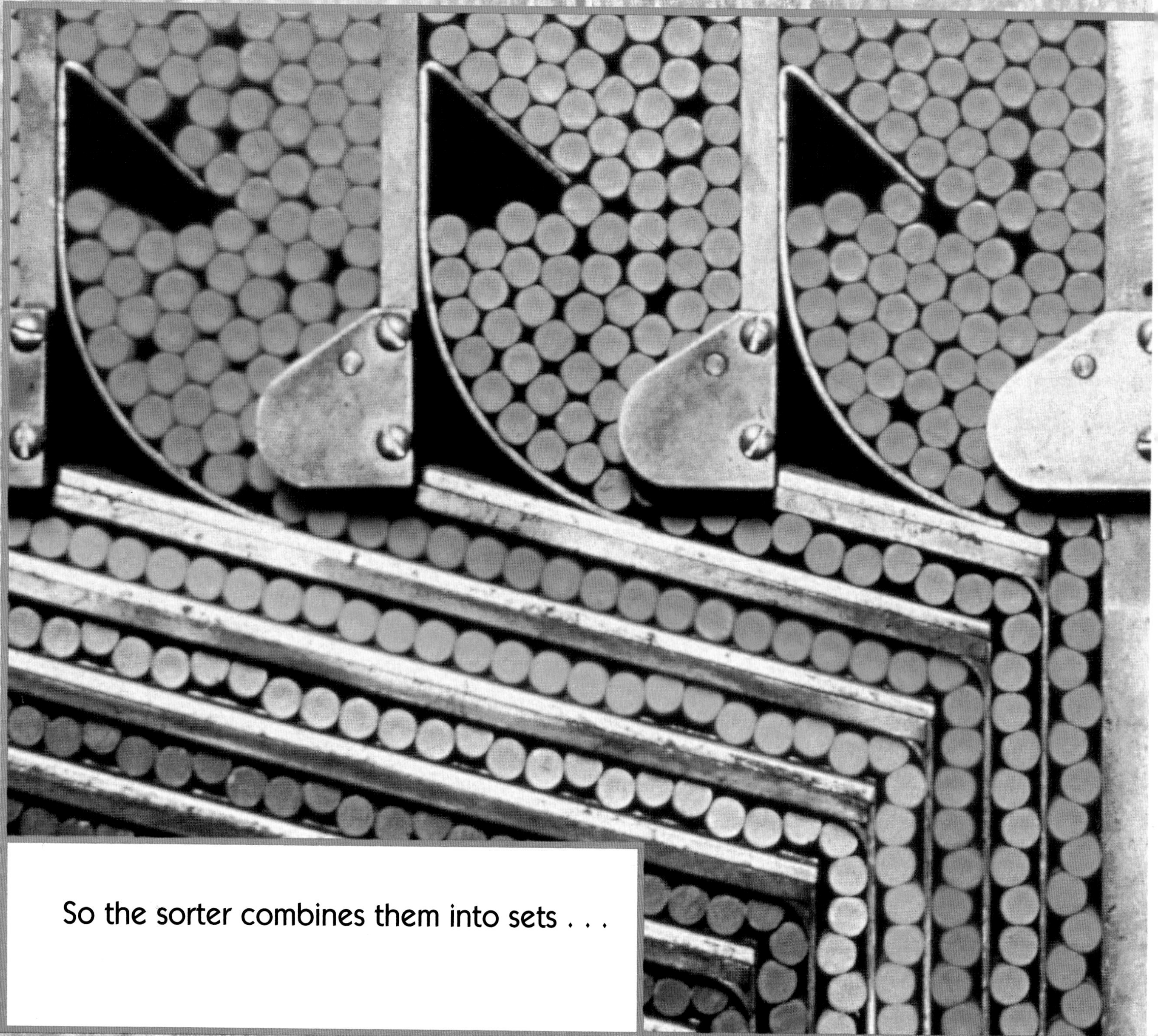

So the sorter combines them into sets . . .

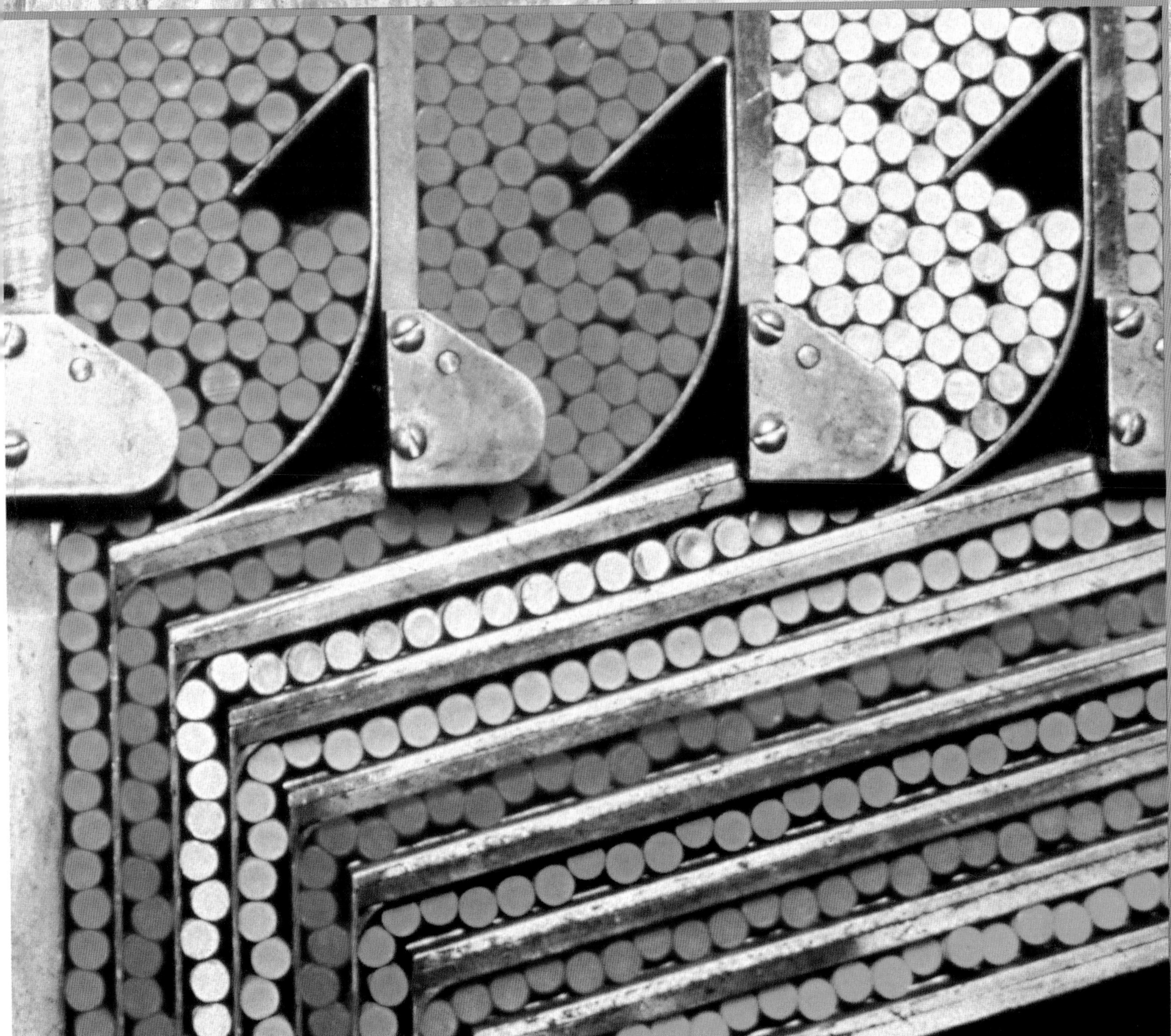

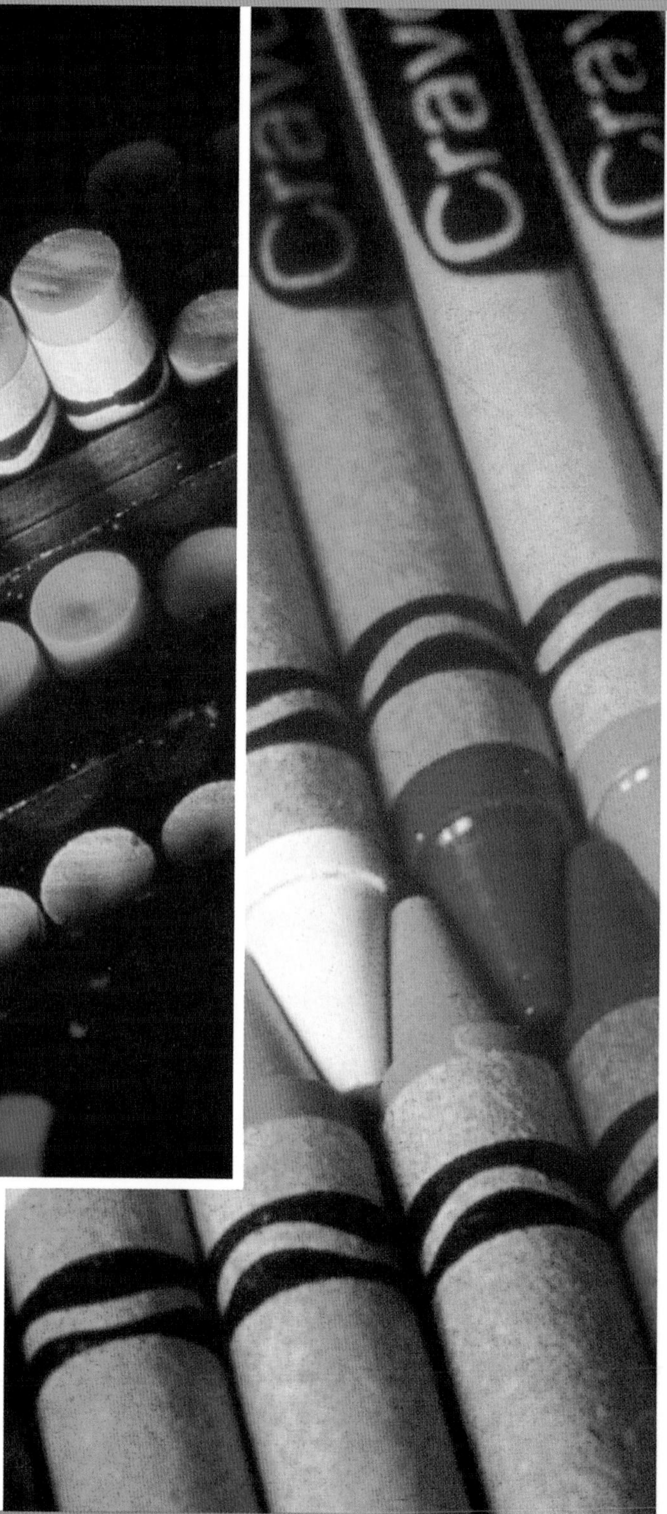

. . . with all the colors that people like to use.

At last, the crayons reach the packing machine. Here, they go into open-ended packages called sleeves . . .

. . . and then into boxes,
ready for you.

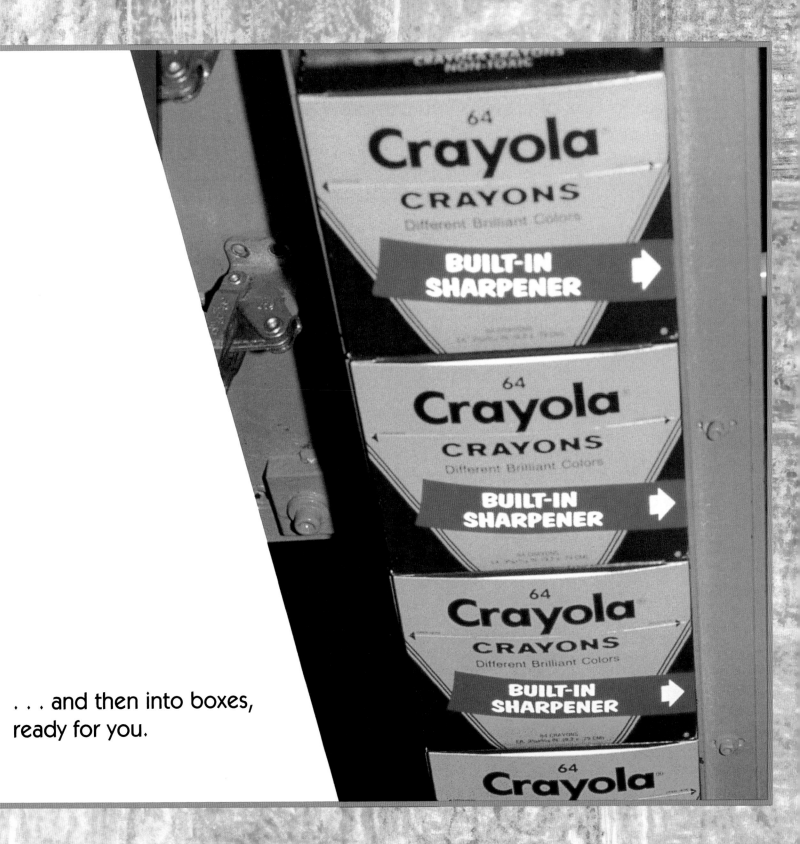

With a good box of crayons you can draw and color just about anything...

. . . even the best-looking person you know.
And who could that be?

Here are some unusual crayon names. Can you think of any others?

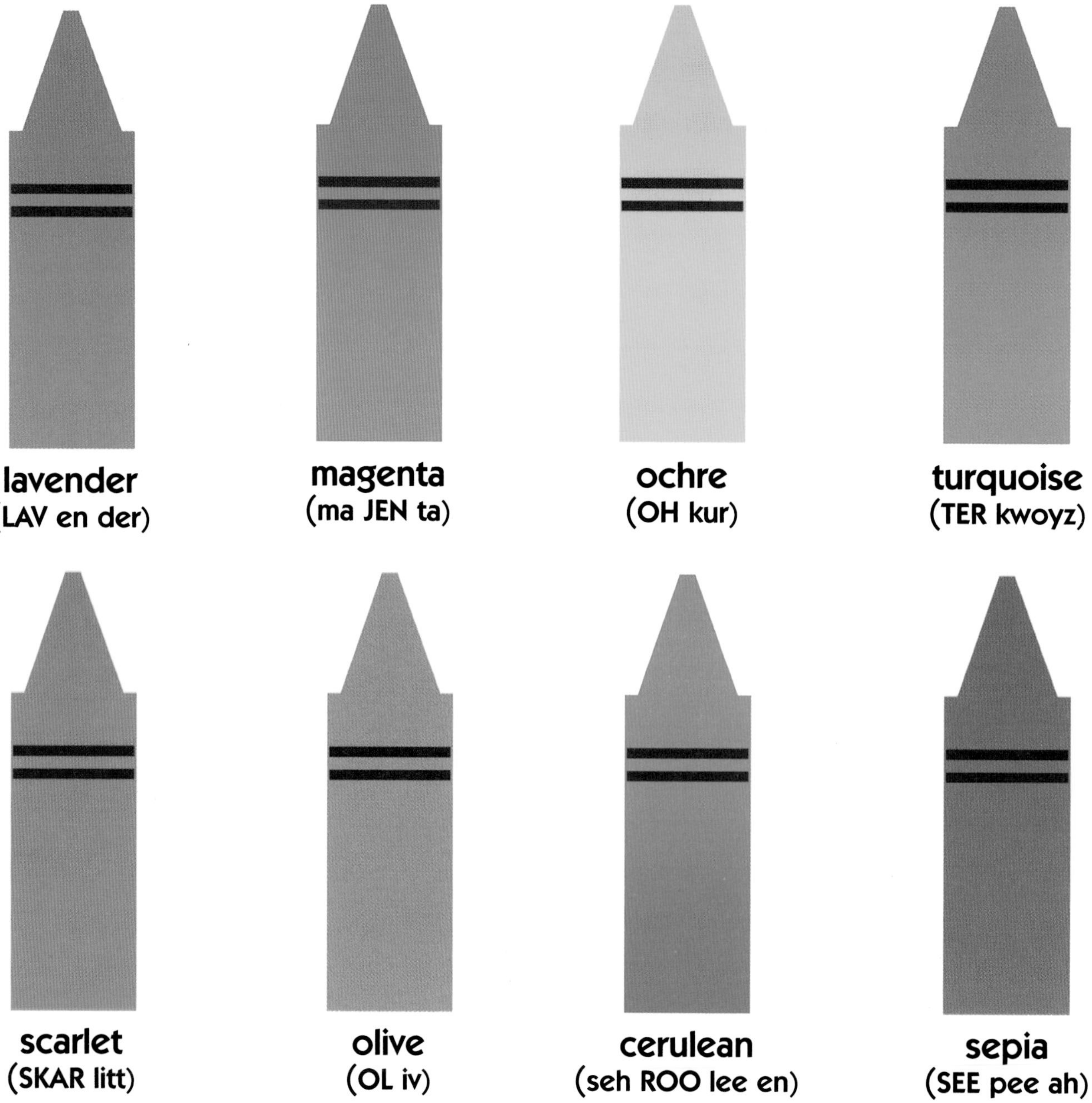

LUNCH LISTS

W9-BIG-118

The cost of each lunch except one adds up to exactly $1.00. Can you find the person who paid more?

CHI-HOON

Cola	$.35
Pita	$.40
Fries	$.25

SASHA

Taco	$.55
Fries	$.45
Water	——

ERNESTO

Salad	$.40
Iced Tea	$.30
Bread Sticks	$.30

FREDRIKA

Chili	$.35
Milk	$.25
Muffin	$.20
Crackers	$.20

ation: Anni Matsick

JULIO

Salad	$.40
Chocolate Milk	$.35
Chips	$.25

LUISA

Soup	$.20
Sandwich	$.20
Milk	$.25
Rice Pudding	$.15
Crackers	$.20

JACQUES

Slice of Pizza	$.30
Chocolate Shake	$.55
Chips	$.25

EVERY VOTE COUNTS

Can you cast a vot
and identify the numbe
described on each sign

Vote
B. I'm greater than 25, less than 40, and divisible by 10.
A. I'm less than 15 and divisible by both 3 and 4.
Vote
Vote
VOTE for ME
C. I'm the only even number between 16 and 23 that is evenly divisible by 3.
D. I'm the smallest number evenly divisible by both 6 and 7.
E. I'm a two-digit number that is less than 25 and evenly divisible by 9.

Which number is nominated on the most posters?

G. The number after me that is also evenly divisible by 11 is 66.

F. When I'm doubled, I'm two less than 60.

I. If you add me to myself seven times, you get the lowest odd number between 61 and 69.

H. I'm the second-smallest number evenly divisible by both 6 and 7.

K. I'm ten less than 100 when multiplied by 5.

J. I'm the first number you can count to that is evenly divisible by all the even numbers below 8.

Answer on page 48

Hint on page 46

Illustration: Diana Zourelias

SIMONE SAYS

When Simone folds this figure together, which one of the four choices will it look like?

Answer on page 48

SALMON SWIM

This salmon is freezing at the southern end of Runaway River. It's in 8° water and wants to reach 80°, but it can only count up by 8s as it moves. Help the salmon swim upstream to warmer waters.

Answer on page 48

Illustration: Don Robison

HANDS OFF

Today was the new clockmaker's first hands-on experience, and he got a little mixed up. He switched the positions of the big hand and the little hand on each clock. Can you look at each clock and figure out what

time it's supposed to be? Once you figure out the times, read the letter on the sign near each clock in order from midnight to noon. The letters should tell you this new clockmaker's name.

Answer on page 48

AGING APES

The names of the apes in the city zoo can give you the primates' current ages. Each letter in a name stands for a number from 1 to 26 (A=1, B=2, C=3, and so on). Can you determine all the ages and tell which ape is the oldest?

Answer on page 48

Illustration: David Helton

DOTS A LOT

Count by 2s to connect these dots and you'll find an odd way to get around.

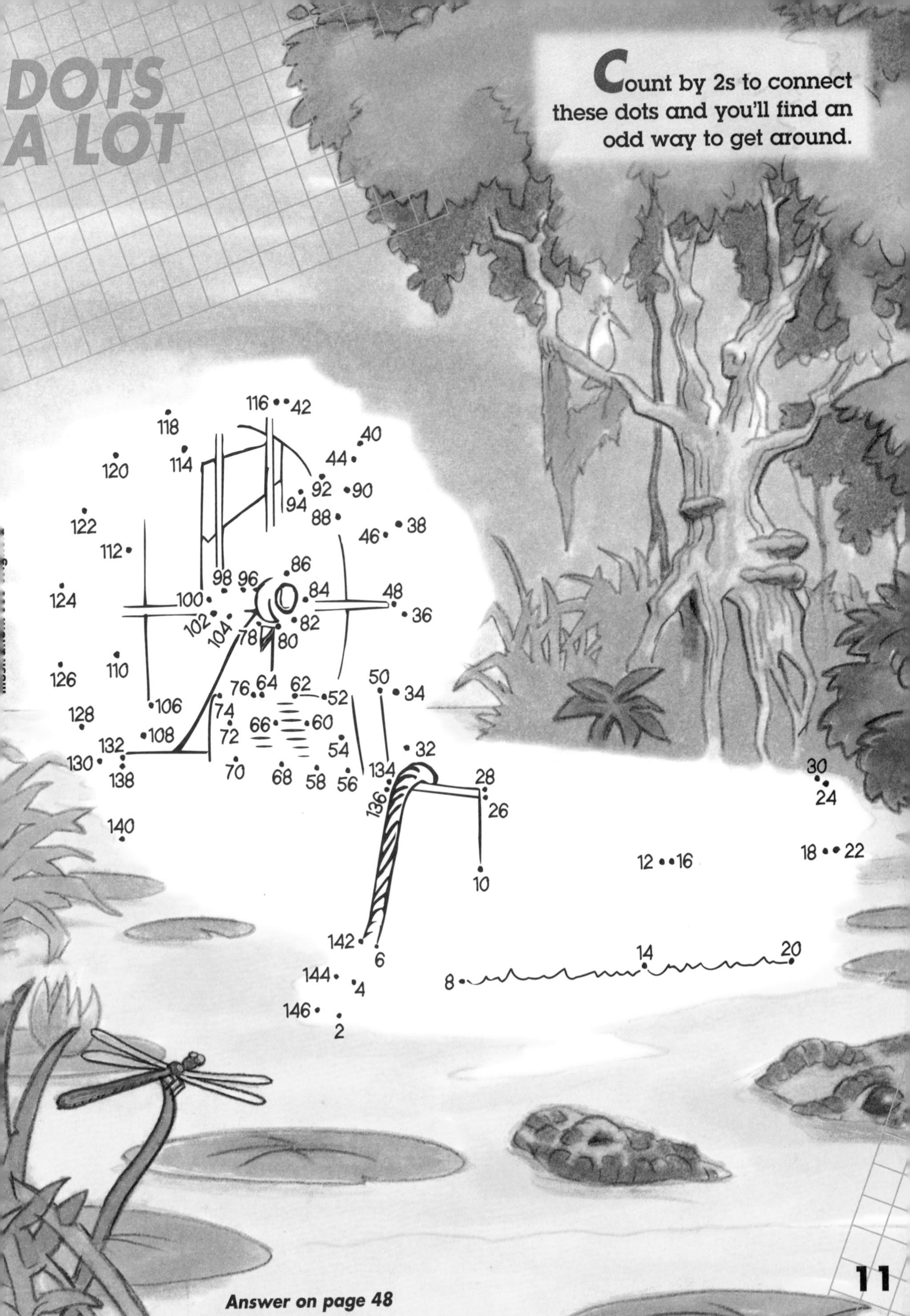

Answer on page 48

QUARTER TIME

When you hear the word *quarter*, you probably think of a coin. But *quarter* is used to describe other things, too. Some are bouncing around here. Read each clue, then try to find the coin with the word that matches.

ACROSS

1. Breed of equine used for short-distance races
4. Every six hours is a quarter of one of these.
5. A military officer responsible for outfitting troops
7. Football position
9. Round in a sports contest before the semifinal
11. The first quarter of this comes between the new one and the full one.
12. A quarter is one of these.
13. This gets one count when the measure of music is in $\frac{4}{4}$ time.

DOWN

1. Fifteen minutes is a quarter of this.
2. *Quarters* describes where a person lives, also known as his or her _____.
3. Three months is a quarter of this.
4. The rear part of a ship's upper level
6. A stout iron-tipped pole
8. Four quarts make one of these.
10. 500 pounds is a quarter of this.
11. 160 acres is a quarter of a square _____.

the clue. The word *quarter* is part of some of the words on the coins. When you find the right word, write it in the boxes in the grid, one letter per box. You should be done in a quarter of the time!

Illustration: R. Michael Palan

Answer on page 48

QUICK FIXES

June 1 was a bad day for Jeff. Six different people came in at the same time with items that needed repair. He jotted down some notes. But he can't figure out the order in which things need to be ready. Can you?

Hint on page 46

1. The television will be ready the last Thursday of the month.
2. The computer will be ready 2 weeks from the day it was brought in.
3. The toaster will be fixed 3 days before the television.
4. The videocassette recorder will be repaired in 6 days.
5. The car will be ready 2 days after it was brought in.
6. The wristwatch will be fixed 4 days after the VCR.

Answer on page 49

FAMOUS NAME

If you connect the dots in the order listed, you will find the name of the person described in this autobiography.

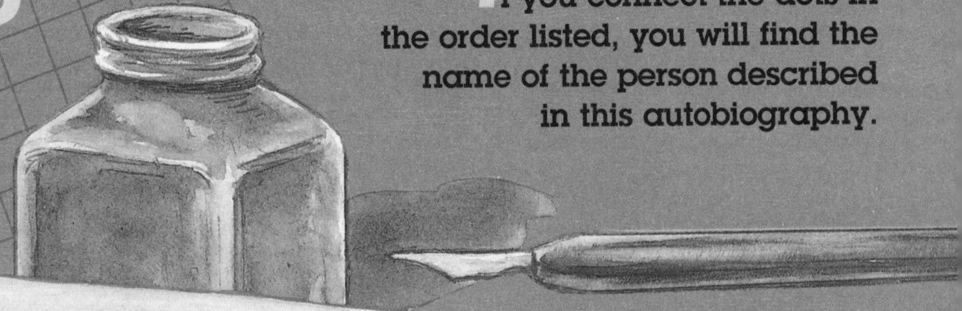

I was born in 1898 in Ukraine. My family moved to Wisconsin when I was eight. I later became a schoolteacher in Wisconsin before moving to what is now Israel. Women were not deeply involved in politics in those days, but I wanted to do all I could to help the new country. I served as the minister of labor, the minister of foreign affairs, the secretary-general of the Labor Party, and finally as prime minister of the entire nation of Israel.

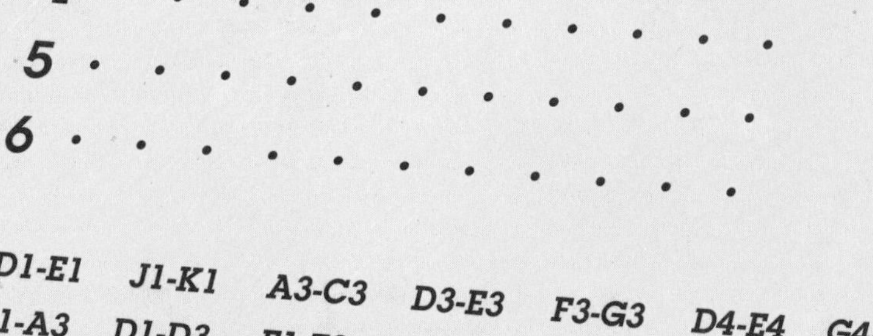

A1-C1 D1-E1 J1-K1 A3-C3 D3-E3 F3-G3 D4-E4 G4-H4
D6-E6 A1-A3 D1-D3 E1-E3 F1-F3 H1-H3 J1-J3 K1-K3
A4-A6 C4-C6 D4-D6 F4-F6 G4-G6 H4-H5 B2-C2 J2-K2
D5-E5 G5-H5 H1-I2 A4-B5 C2-C3 I2-H3 C4-B5 G5-H6

Answer on page 49

Illustration: Kit Wray

LOTS IN COMMON

These kids came to the park in different vans. One van carried four kids, one carried three kids, one carried two, and one van

Hint on page 46

Illustration: Scott Peck

came with only one child. Can you do the problems on each shirt to identify which children came in which van?

nswer on page 49

CARRY THE FOUR

Melissa picked four 12-pound bags of apples. Now she needs to pick out the wagon or wheelbarrow that can hold all her apples on the way home. Do you know which she should choose?

Hint on page 46

 Answer on page 49

RUN FOR FUN

Casey and Dana ran in a 20-mile race to raise money for a local charity. Casey ran at a speed of 8 miles per hour, and Dana ran all her miles in 8 minutes each. Who won the race?

Answer on page 49

ANCIENT AUCTION

That amazing explorer, R. K. Ologest, found these old objects while digging in Africa last year. Several museums have

placed bids as shown on the chart. Write the word *true* or *false* after the statements that describe the bids.

OBJECTS	MONTH FOUND	BIDS		
		This Stonian Museum	Museum of Unnatural Stuff	Vannegie Institute
Painted vase	February	$11,700	$10,900	$12,200
Stone hammer	August	$500	$1,500	$1,900
Wooden wheel	July	$46,800	$61,000	$64,000
Animal-skin shoe	March	$14,750	$13,000	$9,800
Stone bowl	September	$4,900	$6,900	$4,600
Leather pouch	September	$14,000	$15,500	$18,560
Bone necklace	April	$48,100	$31,200	$31,000

1. The highest price offered for the stone bowl is less than the lowest price offered for the bone necklace. ________
2. If all the items are sold for the highest bids offered, the total will be $166,410. ________
3. The museums don't really want the stone hammer. ________
4. The Vannegie Institute offers the greatest sum of money for all the objects. ________
5. The Vannegie Institute offers the highest bids on everything. ________
6. This Stonian Museum has the winning bid on only one item. ________
7. The wooden wheel is the most valuable. ________
8. The museum willing to spend the greatest sum of money for all the objects is This Stonian Museum. ________
9. The object whose bid prices are the closest is the painted vase. ________
10. The painted vase is the first object Mr. Ologest found. ________

Answer on page 49

CALL WAITING

Aunt Matilda is waiting for you to call. The problem is, you can't remember which of the numbers on your list belongs to her. You know her number starts and ends with even numerals, that the area code is 000, and that all of the numbers added together singly equal 38. Which number is Aunt Matilda's?

Answer on page 49

HO-HO-HOLES

To find the solution to our riddle, you need to find the number that belongs in each blank. Each number has a corresponding letter. Place the matching letter in the holes above the right number. When you get all the letters, you'll know the answer. Work the problems moving from left to right, one missing number at a time.

Why did the math teacher's plants come up so straight?

2 + 2 = ___ + 7 = ___ – ___ = 2 + ___ =

1-L	7-U
2-O	8-Q
3-S	9-E
4-T	10-D
5-A	11-H
6-Y	12-R

8 – 3 = ___ – ___ = 4 – ___ =

3 + 8 = ___ – 6 = ___ + ___ =

15 – ___ = 12 – ___ = 4 + ___ = 11 – 6 = ___ + 7 = ___ – ___ =

3 + ___ = 15 – ___ = 13 – 11 = ___ + ___ = 6 – 3 = ___.

Answer on page 49

SCRAMBLED PICTURE

Copy these mixed-up rectangles onto the next page to unscramble the scene.

A-3   A-2   A-4   A-1

B-4   B-1   B-3   B-2

C-3   C-2   C-1   C-4

D-4   D-1   D-3   D-2

The letters and numbers tell you where each rectangle belongs. We've done the first one, A-3, to start you off.

	1	2	3	4
A				
B				
C				
D				

Illustration: Joe Wigfield

Answer on page 50

DIGIT DOES IT

That super sleuth, Inspector Digit, was hot on the trail of a penny-ante coin thief. Digit was walking the floor of the coin convention when an entire display of coins

Answer on page 50

crashed to the ground. The only clue to the crash was a note. Can you decipher it and help the Inspector gather the evidence?

Illustration: Joe Boddy

Hint on page 47

ALL EQUAL

Hint on page 47

In grid A, the numerals in each row equal the number in the purple circle at the end. The numerals in each column equal the number in the purple circle at the bottom. In grid B, work the numbers in the opposite direction. Can you fill in the missing numbers, using only single digits?

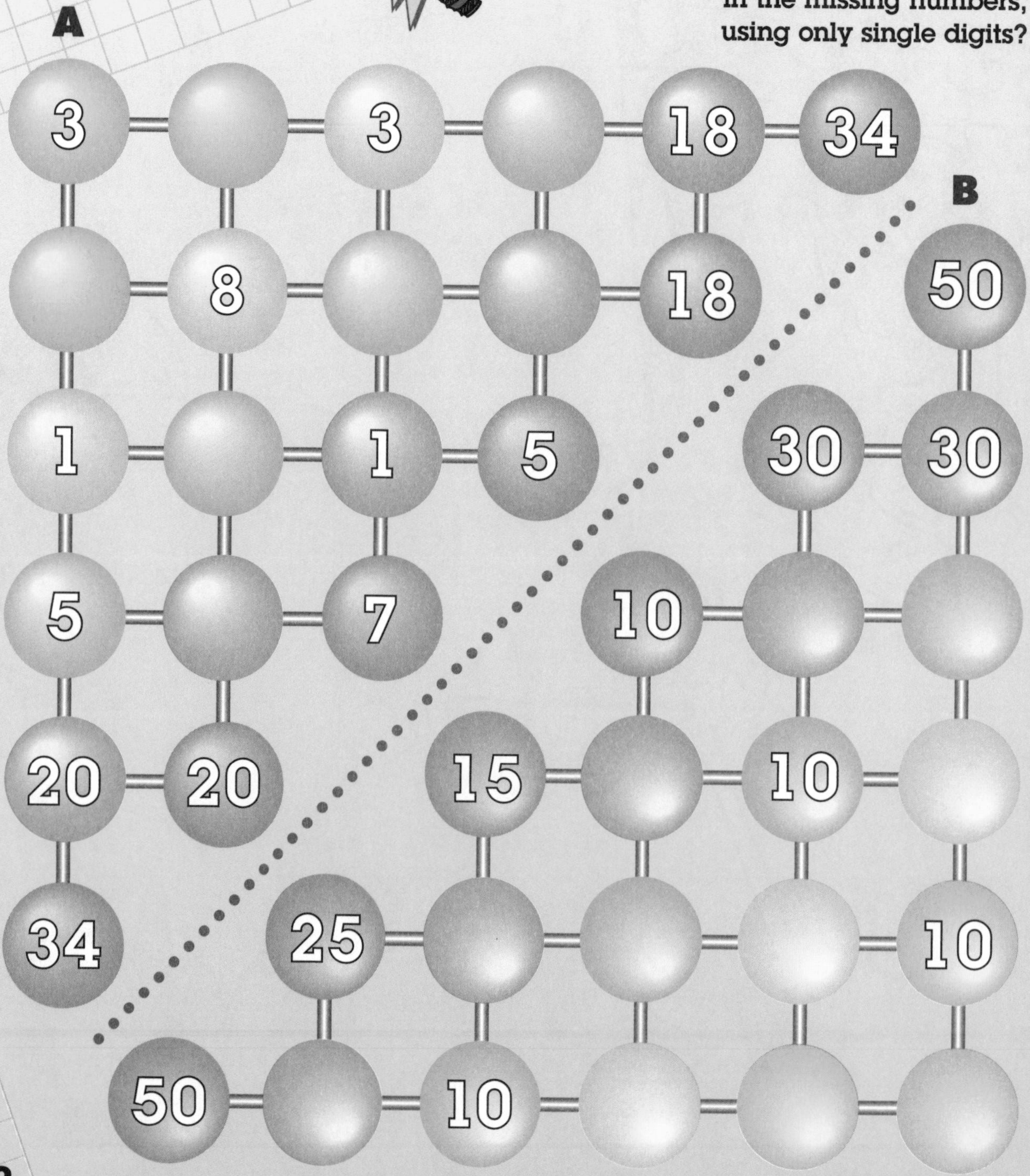

Answer on page 50

TENTH TIME

This board is marked off in ten equal sections. Each section is lettered. To solve our riddle, check the fractions below each blank. That will tell you which fraction of the board to look at for the correct letter, going from left to right.

Illustration: David Helton

What did the sign on the chicken coop say?

Hint on page 47

__ __ __ __ __   __ __   __ __ __ __ __.

$\frac{8}{10}$ $\frac{6}{10}$ $\frac{6}{10}$ $\frac{9}{10}$ $\frac{10}{10}$ $\frac{4}{10}$ $\frac{5}{10}$ $\frac{7}{10}$ $\frac{3}{10}$ $\frac{1}{10}$ $\frac{2}{10}$ $\frac{3}{10}$

Answer on page 50

OVERDUE

The kids in Tome Town use the library a lot. Unfortunately, they love books so much, they sometimes forget to return

Hint on page 47

them in time. Can you help Miss Information calculate how much each child owes for the books he or she is returning?

OVERDUE	AMOUNT OWED PER BOOK PER DAY
1-7 days	$.05
8-30 days	$.10
31-60 days	$.15

After 60 days, a book is declared lost.
Please note: The longer a book is overdue, the more expensive the daily charges.

Illustration: R. Michael Palan

Answer on page 50

LIBRARY LAUGHS

Dewey has some funny books in his library. To check one out, solve each problem. Then go to the shelves to find the volume with the number that matches each answer. Put the matching letter in the blank beside each answer. Read down the letters you've filled in to find the title and author of the book Dewey just finished reading.

27 ÷ 9 = ___ ___
4 – 3 = ___ ___
4 x 5 = ___ ___
21 ÷ 7 = ___ ___
6 + 2 = ___ ___
5 + 4 = ___ ___
7 x 2 = ___ ___
14 ÷ 2 = ___ ___
25 – 2 = ___ ___
10 + 5 = ___ ___
19 – 1 = ___ ___
8 + 5 = ___ ___
16 + 3 = ___ ___
8 – 6 = ___ ___
5 x 5 = ___ ___
25 ÷ 5 = ___ ___
19 – 18 = ___ ___
6 x 3 = ___ ___
36 ÷ 3 = ___ ___
21 – 16 = ___ ___
10 ÷ 5 = ___ ___
3 x 3 = ___ ___
36 ÷ 2 = ___ ___
2 + 2 = ___ ___

Hint on page 47

Answer on page 50

PRECISE ICE

Re-create this image without crossing over any lines or removing your pencil from the page.

Answer on page 50

Illustration: Barbara Gray

COLLECTORS' CLUB

To join the Collectors' Club, you can collect any item you want, but you must have 1,000 or more of that item.

Daniella
DRIED FLOWERS
- Started with 5,817
- Donated 1,720 for school play
- Threw 112 in family pool for party decorations

Mike—PIECES OF CHALK
- Started with 2,960 pieces
- Gave 95 to schoolmates
- Used up 787 pieces
- Accidentally stepped on another 12

Julie—WATER BOTTLES
- Started with 560
- Bought 700 at yard sales
- Drank 182 full bottles of water and gave them to the recycling center

Dara—MARBLES
- Started with 1,030
- Lost 25
- Dropped 4 behind sink

Kevin—SPORTS CAPS
- Started with 4,851
- Gave 2,300 to children's hospital

Answer on page 50

Can you tell which collectors are eligible for membership? Which collector has no items left?

Drew—MOVIE POSTERS
- Started with 200
- Found 2,842 at yard sales
- Gave 1,950 to museum
- Accidentally ripped 94

Randi—PICTURE FRAMES
- Started with 945
- Donated 31 to charity
- Gave 40 to family members

Rachel—CAT FIGURINES
- Started with 1,000 figurines
- Broke half of them
- Inherited 600 from a great-grandmother

Seth—BUMPER STICKERS
- Started with 5,007
- Sold 1,200 at auto show
- Gave 3,600 to other collectors
- Stuck 207 on brother's bedroom wall

Darren—SCREWDRIVERS
- Started with 3,804
- Wore out 426
- Lost 2,900 during a move

ERNIE'S ERRANDS

Ernie wrote down a list of appointments and errands he needs to do today. When he wrote out his list, he estimated how long it would take to accomplish each task. Will he be able to do everything before he has to pick up his daughter?

DENTIST TODAY!
DAD-- PICK ME UP-2:00 DON'T FORGET -J
DEPOSIT
MILK CHEESE EGGS BREAD CATSUP TOOTH-PASTE CAKE!!
Bank: 15 minutes
Library: 20 minutes
Dry cleaners: 10 minutes
Dentist: 45 minutes
Lunch with friend: 1 hour
Barber: 1 hour
Grocery store: 45 minutes
Bakery: 15 minutes
Pick up Jacquie at 2:00.

Illustration: Ron Zalme

Hint on page 47

Answer on page 50

VENN AGAIN

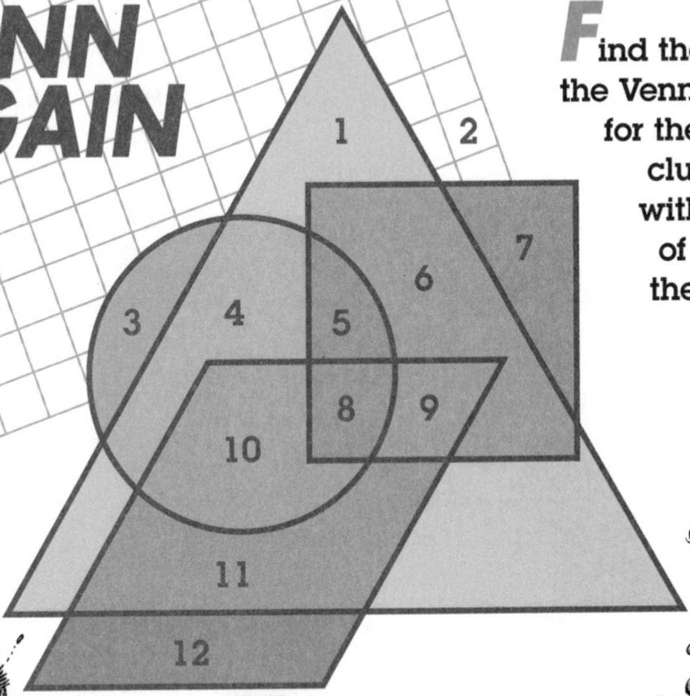

Find the answer to the riddle using the Venn diagram shown here. Look for the number described in each clue. Then match that number with the letter at the beginning of the clue. Write that letter in the blank above the matching number. The first one has been done to start you off.

E—In the □, but in no other shape: 7

O—In all the shapes except the ○: ______

A—In the △ and ○, but not in the □ or ▱: ______

Y—In the ▱, but in no other shape: ______

E—In none of the shapes: ______

W—In all the shapes except the ▱: ______

T—In the △, but in no other shape: ______

L—In the △ and □, but not in the ○ or ▱: ______

D—In all four shapes: ______

S—In the △ and ▱, but not in the ○ or □: ______

R—In the ○, but in no other shape: ______

G—In the △, ▱, and ○, but not in the □: ______

What does the starter say at the beginning of a firefly race?

__ E __ __ __, __ __ __, __ __ __ __!

3 7 4 8 12   11 2 1   10 6 9 5

Answer on page 50

PATTERN PLAY

Tracy wrote a number of sill sentences. Her favorite item ir a different category is hidder in each sentence. The item may b hidden in the first letter of ever word in the sentence, or mayb

Hint on page 47

Sentence

1. Can apes open plastic seals?
2. Wave this phone wildly amid dinner.
3. Odd coats still possess style.
4. The bad two skis.
5. Trembling, strange cattle rushed.
6. Please harpoon directly postcards mailed eagerly.
7. Old muscles know achy pharmacists.
8. Giggle more when seeing monsters.
9. Peaceful areas along straight roads remain.
10. How tricky can little ideas turn?
11. The wild elephants left Vermont early.
12. Aces that win accept payment against losses.

it's in the second, third, fourth, or fifth letter of every word. Her favorites are not related to the actual sentences or questions. Can you find the favorite in each sentence? One is done for you.

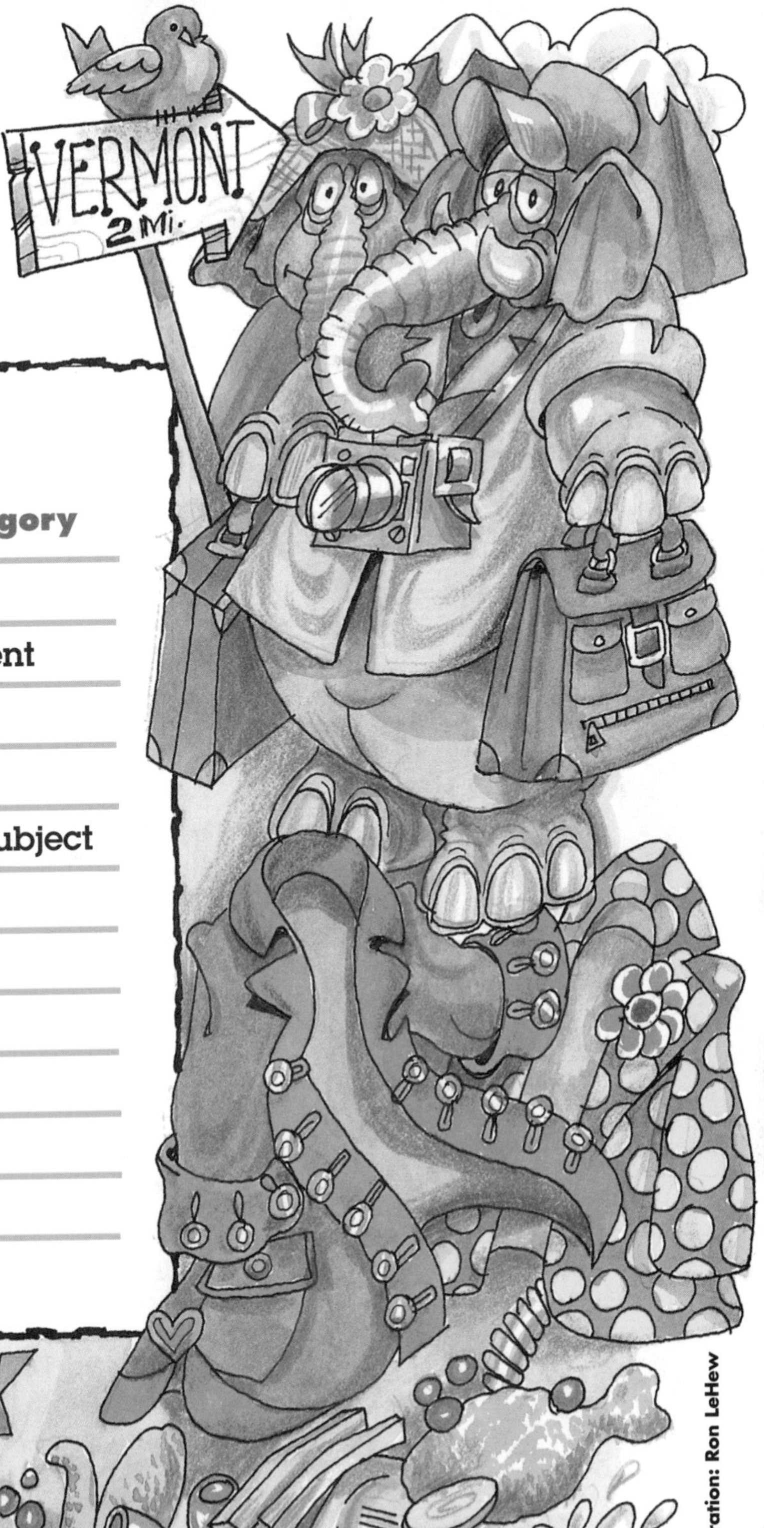

	Hidden Word	Which Letter?	Category
	apple	2nd	Fruit
			Instrument
			Flower
			Bird
			School subject
			Sport
			Meal
			Color
			Country
			Season
			Number
			City

Illustration: Ron LeHew

Answer on page 51

WATER LOG

Arlene is keeping a journal for her health class. This week, she has to keep track of the number of glasses of water she drinks each day for a week. Her teacher recommended that each student should drink at least a $\frac{1}{4}$ of a gallon of water a day for a total of 224 ounces for the week. Can you tell how many ounces of water Arlene drank each day? What was her total intake of water for the week? How many days did she get at least the recommended $\frac{1}{4}$ gallon?

Hint on page 47

Illustration: Doug Cushman

COLOR BY NUMBERS

Shade in all the spaces which have answers that equal 12 before this picture takes its toll.

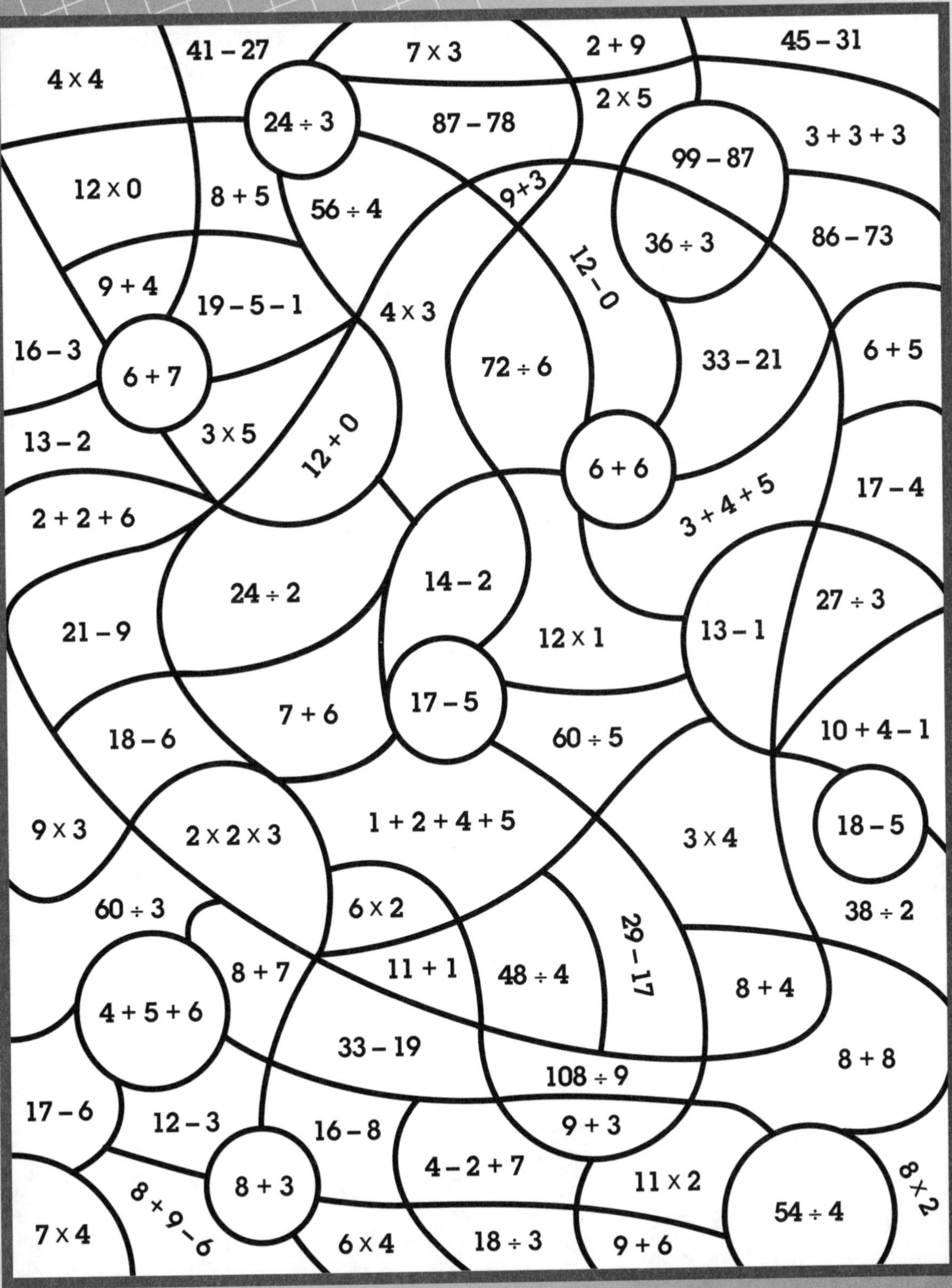

Answer on page 51

CROSSWORD RIDDLE

Fill in these boxes with the letters of the words that answer each clue or description. When you've completed the grid, rearrange the letters in the yellow boxes to discover the answer to our riddle.

ACROSS

1. Days in a week
5. Abbreviation for *Alabama*
6. 1 Across in roman numerals
8. 10:10 written out
10. 5th and 6th letters of the alphabet
12. IX – III
13. Abbreviation for *television*
14. Abbreviation for *number*, or opposite of *yes*
15. Last two letters of 8 Across
16. 2nd and 3rd vowels
17. Roadway through a mountain or under a river
20. Abbreviation for *years*
21. The odds are a million ____ one.
22. 16 ounces make one of these.

DOWN

1. The first septuagenarian year
2. Very large pot
3. 132 months equal this many years.
4. 1 Across in Spanish
6. Abbreviation for *Vermont*
7. Asked to attend a party
9. 11:51 or ____ ____ midnight
11. A dog walks on all ____.
18. The letters at the top and bottom of a compass
19. Short form of *Louis*

Answer on page 51

Hint on page 47

Illustration: Rick Geary

It's the last thing every teenager is:

__ __ __ __ __ __ __ __ __ .

HOT SHOTS

Stacie Stats is trying to figure out the field goal percentage for each basketball player. This percentage compares the number of shots a player takes to the number of shots that actually go in the basket.

Hint on page 47

Stacie has a formula that lets her find the percentages.

1. Divide the number of baskets made by the total number of shots taken.
2. Move the decimal point 2 places to the right.

For example, Josie Sinkit made 20 baskets, taking 40 shots (20 ÷ 40 = .50). Move the decimal point to get 50%.

Can you help Stacie fill in the rest of her chart? Which player has the best shooting percentage?

PLAYER	BASKETS MADE	SHOTS TAKEN	PERCENTAGE
Ella Swish	18	60	
Sam Dunk	10	25	
Frea Throw	24	40	
Pam Poms	30	60	
Mia Pass	16	20	
Ima Player	28	40	
Donna Dribble	6	30	
Theresa Pointer	18	30	
Billie Bucket	27	30	

Answer on page 51

BONUS QUESTION

Twelve teams entered this basketball tournament. If each team plays until it is defeated once, how many games will be scheduled in the tournament?

Illustration: Jerry Zimmerman

HINTS AND BRIGHT IDEAS

These hints may help with some of the trickier puzzles.

COVER

Divide the number of pedals by 2 to get the total number of bicycles and tricycles. Then subtract the number of pedals from the number of wheels. This will give you the number of tricycles.

EVERY VOTE COUNTS **(pages 4-5)**

Here are the only numbers running for office: 9, 12, 18, 29, 30, 42, 55, and 84.

HANDS OFF **(pages 8-9)**

Remember to switch the two hands before writing in the time. It might help to redraw the hands on each clock.

QUARTER TIME **(pages 12-13)**

When trying to think of some answers, be sure to include the word *quarter*, as in *quarter horse* and *quarterback*.

QUICK FIXES **(page 14)**

The car will be ready first, the television last. Write the names of the six items on slips of paper. Then move them around to find the right order.

LOTS IN COMMON **(pages 16-17)**

One group has problems that all equal 23. You may want to use a calculator.

CARRY THE FOUR **(page 18)**

Each pound equals 16 ounces. To change pounds to ounces, multiply 16 by the number of pounds. To find the total number of ounces of Melissa's apples, multiply the number of bags by the weight.

DIGIT DOES IT (pages 26-27)

The word *Inspector* appears in the note's greeting. Use the code numbers from this word to help figure out the rest of the message.

ALL EQUAL (page 28)

Find the numbers for each circle by working in both directions, across and down. Look for the circles that can have only one possible number and fill them in first. Numbers may be repeated more than once in any line.

TENTH TIME (page 29)

To save time, number the sections from $\frac{1}{10}$ to $\frac{10}{10}$ from left to right. To find a spot that is $\frac{8}{10}$ths of the way across, count over 8 spots.

OVERDUE (pages 30-31)

If a book is 30 days overdue, it will cost $3.00 to return it (30 days × $.10 per day = $3.00). If the book is just one more day overdue, the charge jumps up to $4.65 (31 days × $.15 per day = $4.65).

LIBRARY LAUGHS (page 32)

Remember to consult the books to find the letter that matches each number.

ERNIE'S ERRANDS (page 36)

Look at the picture for a clue to the time Ernie is starting out.

PATTERN PLAY (pages 38-39)

For sentence 2, try every third letter.

WATER LOG (page 40)

It takes 4 glasses to get 32 ounces.

CROSSWORD RIDDLE (pages 42-43)

Compass points include north and south. A *vat* is a pot. VII and *siete* are two other ways to write 1 Across.

HOT SHOTS (pages 44-45)

You may want to use a calculator to get the percentages. For the bonus: After the first round, six teams will be eliminated.

ANSWERS

COVER
51 bicycles, 17 tricycles

LUNCH LISTS (page 3)
Jacques paid $1.10.

EVERY VOTE COUNTS (pages 4-5)
A. 12 D. 42 G. 55 J. 12
B. 30 E. 18 H. 84 K. 18
C. 18 F. 29 I. 9
18 is nominated on three different posters.

SIMONE SAYS (page 6)

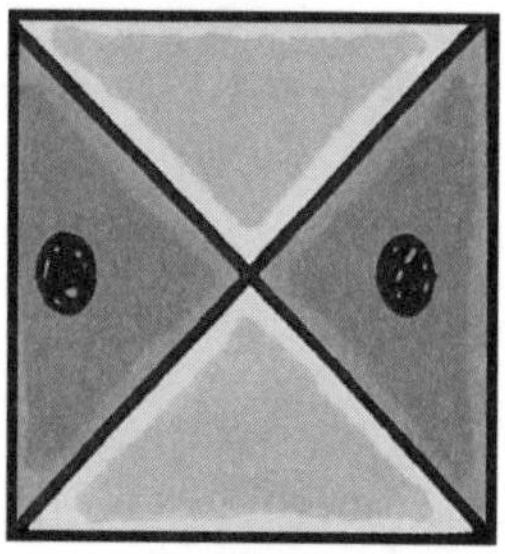

SALMON SWIM (page 7)

HANDS OFF (pages 8-9)

1:10—N 2:35—I 3:00—C 4:00—K
6:00—O 7:30—T 8:55—I 9:15—M 11:50—E
The clockmaker's name is NICK O'TIME.

AGING APES (page 10)
WALDO: 23 + 1 + 12 + 4 + 15 = 55
FELIX: 6 + 5 + 12 + 9 + 24 = 56
ELIZA: 5 + 12 + 9 + 26 + 1 = 53
HILDY: 8 + 9 + 12 + 4 + 25 = 58
GORDO: 7 + 15 + 18 + 4 + 15 = 59
Gordo is the oldest.

DOTS A LOT (page 11)

QUARTER TIME (pages 12-13)

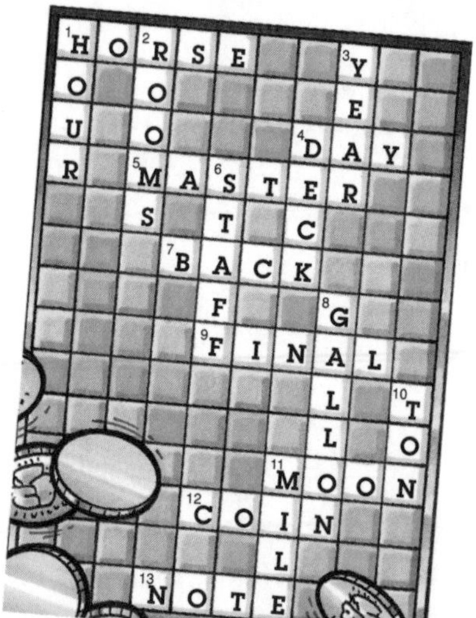

QUICK FIXES (page 14)

The items will be ready in this order:
1. Car
2. Videocassette recorder
3. Wristwatch
4. Computer
5. Toaster
6. Television

FAMOUS NAME (page 15)

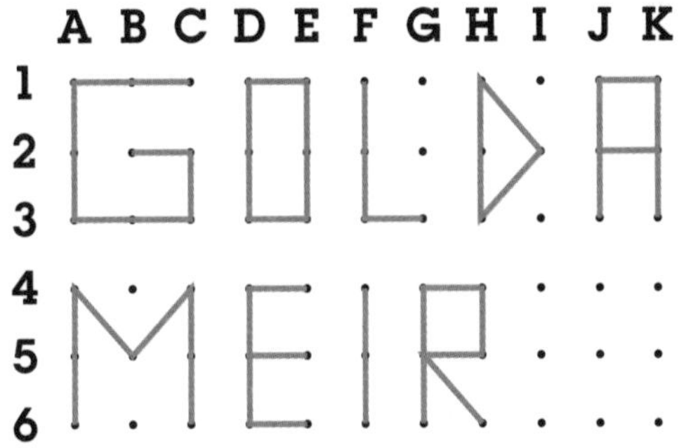

LOTS IN COMMON (pages 16-17)

Van 1:
1,144 ÷ 13 = 88

Van 2:
5,928 ÷ 456 = 13
4,329 ÷ 333 = 13

Van 3:
3,648 ÷ 456 = 8
728 ÷ 91 = 8
1,696 ÷ 212 = 8

Van 4:
2,093 ÷ 91 = 23
10,488 ÷ 456 = 23
1,035 ÷ 45 = 23
2,277 ÷ 99 = 23

CARRY THE FOUR (page 18)

Melissa's bags total 768 ounces.
Wagon D will hold all four bags.
A. 562 ounces
B. 30 pounds × 16 = 480 ounces
C. 725 ounces
D. 768 ounces
E. 45 pounds × 16 = 720 ounces

RUN FOR FUN (page 19)

Casey finished her 20 miles in 2 hours, 30 minutes. Dana ran her 20 miles at 8 minutes each, for a total of 160 minutes or 2 hours, 40 minutes. Casey won.

ANCIENT AUCTION (pages 20-21)

1. TRUE
2. TRUE
3. FALSE. Even though the stone hammer received the lowest bids, the museums still want the object.
4. TRUE. When you add up all the bids from Vannegie Institute, the total is $142,060, which is the most money offered.
5. FALSE. This Stonian Museum offered $14,750 for the shoe and $48,100 for the necklace, and the Museum of Unnatural Stuff offered $6,900 for the bowl. All of these were higher than Vannegie's bids.
6. FALSE. This Stonian Museum has the winning bid on two items: the shoe and the necklace.
7. TRUE
8. FALSE. The Vannegie Institute is willing to spend the greatest sum of money—$142,060.
9. TRUE. If you subtract the lowest bid ($10,900) from the highest bid ($12,200), the difference is $1,300, the smallest difference of all the bids.
10. TRUE

CALL WAITING (page 22)

802-5968

HO-HO-HOLES (page 23)

Why did the math teacher's plants come up so straight?
THEY ALL HAD SQUARE ROOTS.

SCRAMBLED PICTURE (pages 24-25)

DIGIT DOES IT (pages 26-27)

Dear Inspector Digit,
"Coin" you imagine how upset I was to see you? I went head over tails and knocked over the entire display. You can take it as a small victory that I left all 35 coins here.
Nick L.

a-3	e-9	h-17	l-13	o-11	s-16	v-14
c-15	f-5	i-12	m-7	p-4	t-2	w-6
d-19	g-8	k-1	n-20	r-18	u-21	y-10

ALL EQUAL (page 28)

Here are our answers.
You may have found others.

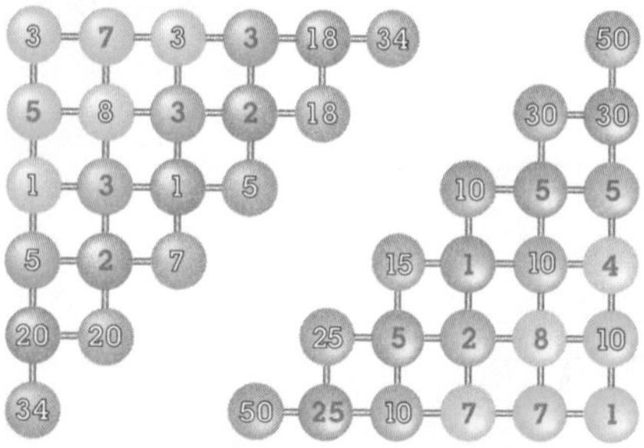

TENTH TIME (page 29)

What did the sign on the chicken coop say?
ROOST IN PEACE.

OVERDUE (pages 30-31)

Pierre	15 × \$.10 = \$1.50 × 2 books = \$3.00
Rory	8 × \$.10 = \$.80
Wallace	30 × \$.10 = \$3.00 × 3 books = \$9.00
Ursula	20 × \$.10 = \$2.00 × 5 books = \$10.00
Xavier	4 × \$.05 = \$.20 × 7 books = \$1.40
Erick	12 × \$.10 = \$1.20 × 4 books = \$4.80
Zoe	29 × \$.10 = \$2.90
Samuel	7 × \$.05 = \$.35 × 10 books = \$3.50
Yolanda	5 × \$.05 = \$.25 × 3 books = \$.75
Victoria	37 × \$.15 = \$5.55 × 2 books = \$11.10

LIBRARY LAUGHS (page 32)

27 ÷ 9 = 3	C	8 – 6 = 2	B
4 – 3 = 1	A	5 × 5 = 25	Y
4 × 5 = 20	T	25 ÷ 5 = 5	E
21 ÷ 7 = 3	C	19 – 18 = 1	A
6 + 2 = 8	H	6 × 3 = 18	R
5 + 4 = 9	I	36 ÷ 3 = 12	L
7 × 2 = 14	N	21 – 16 = 5	E.
14 ÷ 2 = 7	G	10 ÷ 5 = 2	B
25 – 2 = 23	W	3 × 3 = 9	I
10 + 5 = 15	O	36 ÷ 2 = 18	R
19 – 1 = 18	R	2 + 2 = 4	D
8 + 5 = 13	M		
16 + 3 = 19	S		

CATCHING WORMS
by Earl E. Bird

PRECISE ICE (page 33)

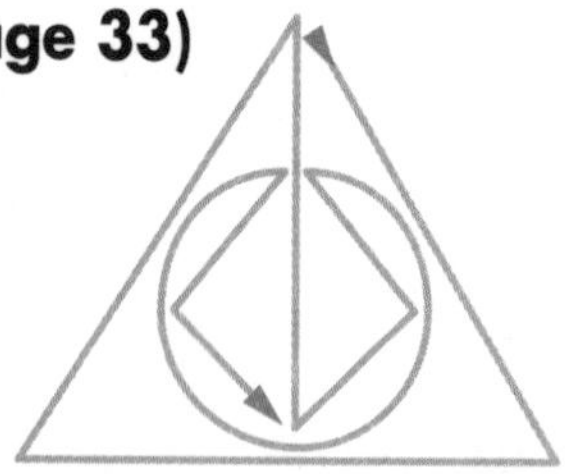

COLLECTORS' CLUB (pages 34-35)

All these people made it into the club:

Mike	2,960 – 95 – 787 – 12 = 2,066
Rachel	1,000 – 500 + 600 = 1,100
Dara	1,030 – 25 – 4 = 1,001
Daniella	5,817 – 1,720 – 112 = 3,985
Julie	560 + 700 – 182 = 1,078
Kevin	4,851 – 2,300 = 2,551

These people had fewer than 1,000 items:

Darren	3,804 – 426 – 2,900 = 478
Randi	945 – 31 – 40 = 874
Drew	200 + 2,842 – 1,950 – 94 = 998

Seth has no items:
5,007 – 1,200 – 3,600 – 207 = 0

ERNIE'S ERRANDS (page 36)

Ernie won't make it. All his errands will take $4\frac{1}{2}$ hours. If he leaves right now, he won't be finished until 2:30.

VENN AGAIN (page 37)

E. 7	E. 2	D. 8
O. 9	W. 5	S. 11
A. 4	T. 1	R. 3
Y. 12	L. 6	G. 10

What does the starter say at the beginning of a firefly race?
READY, SET, GLOW!